A journey *of*

A PILGRIM'S GUIDE TO PRAYER

Kate Hayes

A journey of the heart: A PILGRIM'S GUIDE TO PRAYER

An individual or small group Bible resource from Scripture Union

Published by Scripture Union, 207–209 Queensway, Bletchley, MK2 2EB, England.

Scripture Union Australia: Locked Bag 2, Central Coast Business Centre, NSW 2252. www.su.org.au

Scripture Union: We are an international Christian charity working with churches in more than 130 countries providing resources to bring the good news about Jesus Christ to children, young people and families – and to encourage them to develop spiritually through the Bible and prayer. As well as our network of volunteers, staff and associates who run holidays, church-based events and school Christian groups, we produce a wide range of publications and support those who use our resources through training programmes.

Email: info@scriptureunion.org.uk

Internet: www.scriptureunion.org.uk

First published 2003

ISBN 1 85999 797 X

Scripture taken from the New Living Translation, British text, published by Tyndale House Publishers, Inc, Wheaton, Illinois, USA, and distributed by STL Ltd, Carlisle, Cumbria, England.

British Library Cataloguing-in-Publication Data: a catalogue record for this book is available from the British Library.

Cover design by Phil Grundy.

Printed and bound by Interprint of Malta.

The way ahead

*T*his book is a companion to any individual or small group wanting to grow their prayer experience. But think of it more as a map book than a recipe book. No two individuals will have the same prayer journey, though some will find themselves on paths that others have travelled. It's good to meet fellow pilgrims along the way and learn from each other.

Some will be travelling in prayer with light hearts. They are discovering a growing intimacy with the Father they love; they sense they are heard, affirmed, encouraged. They feel a response to the cries of their hearts. They feel answered.

But others seem to be stumbling along a different prayer path. The ground is stony; there are obstructions and diversions. They feel alone, unheard, ignored. Their hearts ache for even a murmur of response. But the silence is deafening. They feel lost, anxious that they have wandered off track.

Take courage! Let us travel together for a while, share our hearts, and seek that answering voice together. It may be that we shall discover other ways of listening, other ways of hearing, and we may find that all the paths are one, and that the diversions and roadblocks are indeed part of the map.

The Solitary Pilgrim

This book is a companion for the solitary traveller. You can work through the material at your own pace, ignoring only those sections marked with the group logo. It may be helpful for you to record your thoughts along the way, either on the pages or in a separate notebook.

The Group of Pilgrims

This book is also a companion for the small group. You may have come together with a Christian friend, as a prayer triplet, as an existing small fellowship group. Or you may be part of a group specially convened for Lent or some other season of the year. Decide whether one person will lead each time you meet, or whether a different person will lead each session. You may want to skip those sections marked with the solitary pilgrim logo.

Using the material

The material is divided into six sessions or chapters. Chapter 1, **On the road**, contains less material, deliberately enabling groups to spend part of their first meeting getting to know one another.

There is a consistent pattern to the material in each session or chapter.

Setting Out will ease you gently into the focus of the session, often with some fun questions. Don't skip this part, even if you are a solitary pilgrim, because however light this material seems it will flag up some important attitudes and preconceptions and will prepare you for deeper exploration of some key issues. Within the group setting, this opening time will develop relationships and encourage honest sharing which will ultimately benefit the group's ease in praying together.

Signposts will take you into the Bible. This time of discovery alone or together will open up a number of lines of thought as you follow through the questions. For groups, this section will particularly facilitate discussion and the sharing of experience.

Prayer is the next section, during which time there is opportunity to pray appropriately and in a way which is directly informed by the session so far. Don't be tempted to rush this; it is not optional but key.

Most chapters contain an **En Route** section. This contains ideas for responses or activities which will not necessarily be completed in the session but over a period of time. These may begin as exercises which, if they prove helpful, may be adopted longer term either in personal or group prayer. Select only what seems helpful to you. For groups this section is something individuals might like to take away and try. But don't forget in subsequent sessions to give opportunity for reporting back.

Finally, there is a **Further Afield** section. This allows further exploration in the Bible. Depending on the length of your times together, groups wanting a longer Bible study section could use some or all of this material in the **Signposts** section. If time is limited, group members might like to take home **Further Afield** for personal study during the week. Individuals can choose to use some or all of this section. Working through it will really add width to your overall experience of **A journey of the heart**.

1 *On the road*

*I*t's the first of six sessions thinking about, looking at, wondering about, exploring prayer. Are you excited, longing to develop your prayer life and get to know God better? Maybe you're sure prayer is a 'good thing' but you've had to steel yourself to 'do your duty' and confront a subject that seems, in all honesty, stupendously boring! If you are meeting with a group, perhaps the panic is rising; this is the moment when everyone else finds out how hopeless your prayer life really is. Possibly you're attending reluctantly. Perhaps you're worried you'll have to pray aloud.

However you're feeling about these sessions, let's face it – prayer can be boring and hard going. It can seem as though our words are bouncing back off the ceiling, pointless mumblings going nowhere. Prayer can be a duty and not a joy. We stumble along with stilted words and clumsy half-sentences, rather than with the flowing poetic and meaningful phrases we wish we could produce.

Most of us sense there should be more to our prayer lives than this. The Bible is full of people who spent time in prayer, not out of duty but out of an overwhelming desire to share the feelings and experiences of the moment with God. More than that, the Bible describes these prayers as making a difference to those who prayed them – a difference that wasn't dependent on the elegance of the language they used or on their confidence with praying aloud, but on their honesty and openness with God.

Setting Out

Q: Did you learn a musical instrument as a child? If so, what did you learn to play? What did you like and dislike most about doing so?

Q: Imagine you have been offered free lessons to learn any instrument of your choice. What would you choose to play? Why?

Through our lifetime we pick up a lot of practical skills, not just musical ones. Perhaps you've learnt to drive, to use a computer, to speak French, to make bread...

Q: What helped you learn these skills?

Q: Are there some things you've tried to learn and given up on? Or avoided altogether? Why?

Q: What made the difference between learning and giving up?

For those of us who weren't born geniuses, musical skills have to be developed. When we first learn to play an instrument we expect it to take lots of hard work before the skilled and fluent playing of the proficient musician grows from our discordant and hesitant beginnings. For some people, prayer comes in the list of things they've learnt how to do and now find relatively straightforward. However, for many if not most of us, it remains a struggle. Sometimes it's erratic: one day it's easy and rewarding, the next we can't even bring ourselves to give it a try. We have to be realistic, not expecting a triumphant prayer life to appear fully formed at the moment of our commitment to Christ. Prayer, like playing the oboe, responds to practice. It is an art form we can develop, a skill we can learn – and yet it is also much more than that.

Q: What do you think would happen to a Christian who never prayed at all?

Q: Can you define in one phrase or sentence what you think is the point of praying?

Not everyone learns to play a musical instrument. Some people don't like music that much, or didn't have the opportunity to learn, or just never saw the point. Whatever the benefits of being able to make music, you can live perfectly well without being able to play – it is not an essential element of life. Prayer, on the other hand, is not just a skill to be learnt if we choose, it is foundational; essential to our relationship with God. We can't leave it to those who are particularly interested in it or naturally find it easy to pray. It is vital for everyone who wants to grow in their relationship with God.

Signposts

Let's look at how prayer makes a difference.

Read

Acts 11:1–18

Q: What was Peter doing when God spoke to him?

Q: What was the point of the vision God gave Peter?

Q: How did the behaviour of Peter and the Church change after this vision?

As Peter prayed, God spoke to him, enabling him to understand more of what God wanted to do; a key moment for the spread of the gospel through the whole world. Our prayers may not have quite such dramatic consequences but, as Peter found, spending time in prayer gives God an opportunity to speak to us. As he does so, we too can grow in our understanding of what God wants to do in the world and the part he wants us to play. Prayer really can change things.

But do we see this happening in practice? By definition, miracles are unusual events and we may not see many events that provide undeniable proof of God at work in a situation. Usually we need faith to see the answers to our prayers.

People around the world prayed for many years for the removal of apartheid in South Africa and for the end of communism in Eastern Europe. For a long time nothing seemed to happen on either of these world stages. Then, apparently very quickly, everything changed. It is impossible to prove that prayer made a difference to those situations. Equally it is impossible to say what would have happened if nobody had prayed at all.

Similarly, when we pray for the more ordinary things of life, perhaps for job interviews, operations or tricky conversations and find things go more smoothly than we feared, are we surprised? Do we trust that God was at work and our prayers did make a difference? Anglican clergyman and reformer William Temple is reported to have said that when he stopped praying, so did coincidences.

Q: Do you believe that prayer makes a difference to world events?

Write down, with today's date, a specific need you have in your life or a specific need you identify in the life of someone you know, and commit yourself to praying on a regular basis for God to answer.

Share specific examples of answered prayer in your group, followed by a prayer of thanksgiving.

Prayer

Spend a few minutes in silence, reflecting on your experiences of prayer up to now.

Consider:

- how you would like your prayer life to develop over the next few weeks.

- how you would like your relationship with God to grow over that time.

Give people an opportunity to share some of their thoughts with each other. End by praying for these things and for one another, either aloud or in silence, as you prefer.

Further Afield

1 WHEN AND WHERE

Read

Matthew 14:22,23

Mark 1:34,35
Luke 5:15,16

These verses record three busy days of preaching, teaching and healing for Jesus – yet days when he still made time and space to pray.

Q: Looking at these verses, when did he make time to pray? And where?

Q: Spending time alone with God in prayer was always a priority for Jesus – never a last resort. Why do you think it was so important for him?

Q: Is spending time in prayer a priority for you at the moment? Why/why not?

Q: Do you have somewhere you go/could go to be alone with him?

Q: When is the best time of day for you to pray?

Q: Is there a step you could take this week to help you spend more time alone with God?

2 FIRST OR LAST

Read

Luke 10:38–42

Mary and Martha both loved Jesus but responded very differently to his visit to their home.

Q: How do *you* behave when you have visitors in your home?

Q: Why didn't Jesus send Mary to help Martha?

Jesus didn't say it was wrong for Martha to provide practical care for her visitors, but that she needed to be sure time with him was at the top of her priority list, above anything else – even serving him.

Q: Do you let work, chores, even church activities, get in the way of spending time with Jesus himself?

Q: How can you make spending time with Jesus your first priority and still fulfil your responsibilities?

3 TO US AND IN US

Read

Acts 4:16–31

The authorities were rattled by the goings on in the young Church and put the believers under pressure to stop preaching about Jesus. The believers came together to pray about the situation.

Q: How would *you* have prayed?

Q: How did the believers begin their prayer?

Q: What did they ask God to do about their problem?

Notice that they didn't ask God to take away the problem but to help them use it for his glory. This doesn't mean that we can't ask God to take away our problems; the Bible describes many occasions when people did just that. However, it does remind us that God doesn't always change what's happening *to* us but what's happening *in* us instead, giving us the strength and help we need to serve him.

2 *Praying on my own*

Setting Out

Are you good at small talk? Do you enjoy chatting to your family, your colleagues, the people at the bus stop or in the supermarket queue about anything and nothing? About the weather, the traffic and last-night's TV? How do you think they'd react if you started talking about prayer? Quite likely they'd think you were weird and pretty embarrassing!

And yet... they've probably given it a go at some point! When? How about that scary moment when the tyre burst on the motorway? Or when someone they loved was very ill?

When we're desperate we try anything, even crying out to God for help and trying to bargain with him: 'If you save us then I'll never say anything nasty again/stop smoking/go and work for a charity...'. Afterwards, if everything works out, usually the promise is forgotten and the prayer brushed off as a moment of weakness. If it doesn't work out then it's proof that God either doesn't exist or doesn't care. How's that for a great introduction to prayer? For most people their only other experiences are the prayers of formal services such as a funeral or a child's christening. No wonder prayer doesn't often have a positive image!

Is this really all that prayer is about? If so, then why does the Bible treat it as such an essential part of a Christian's life? And if it's so important, why do we find it so difficult to do?

Let's start with a dose of hard reality.

To what extent do you agree with the following statements? Mark each 1 to 5, where

0 = I never feel like this
1 = very rarely
2 = sometimes
3 = at least half the time
4 = almost always
5 = every time

___ Starting to pray is a problem for me.

___ When I'm praying on my own I find it hard to know what to say.

___ I pray for the same things every day.

___ Every time I start to pray, something interrupts me.

___ If someone asks me to pray for something, I never remember until I see them again.

___ I don't pray unless I'm in church or it's an emergency.

When everyone has had a few minutes to think about their responses, discuss your answers together.

Think back over the time that you've been a Christian, whether that happened gradually over a period of time or at a particular time. This might be a long time ago, or relatively recently. Spend a few moments in quiet, reflecting on your prayer life over that time, and considering in what ways it has changed.

Q: When was the 'best' time in your prayer life so far – perhaps when it was easiest to pray, or most rewarding?

Q: Have there been times when prayer has been especially hard for you, perhaps impossible? Why do you think that was?

Q: How did you feel towards God in these different times?

Signposts

Read

2 Chronicles 7:14,15

Philippians 4:6,7

Q: What good things, according to these verses, come from prayer?

Q: Can you think of any other benefits?

Prayer builds our relationship with the living God, increasing the degree of intimacy we have with him. If we don't pray then we risk the relationship suffering and becoming distant. If we do pray then we give ourselves the chance to experience all the benefits of a closer relationship with him.

THREE PROBLEMS WITH PRAYER

1 Anything but that

Even when we are sure that prayer is 'a good thing' that will bring us great benefits, most of us still tend to avoid it. We use a variety of excuses to explain our failure to pray.

How could you encourage a Christian friend to pray who says:

I'm too busy to pray.
Mark 1:35; Luke 6:12; 10:41,42

I manage quite well without praying.
John 15:5

I'm too ashamed / not good enough to pray.
Ezra 9:6; Psalm 51

I don't feel anyone is listening when I pray.
Psalm 55:17; Isaiah 40:27–31

My prayers don't work.
Psalms 17:6; 116:1

Q: What excuse (not necessarily one of these) are you most likely to give as a reason for not praying?

Whatever excuses we give for our failure to pray as often and as purposefully as we should, the main reason we don't pray is sin. Sin builds a barrier between us and God. Our inner selves don't want to meet the holy God who hates that sin and wants to weed it out, so we face a battle to begin praying and, once started, have to battle to keep going.

2 Mental drift

'Dear Lord, I thank you that I can come into your presence through the gift of prayer. I wonder where I left my door key? (No, No! Stay on the point.) Heavenly Father, I begin by asking you to watch over Margaret today. That meeting tonight is going to be really boring. What time will I have to put the oven on for tea? (NO, NO!) Please encourage those working for you overseas, especially those people I heard about yesterday in church – from Michael and 'whatsisname' in the bright red shirt. I mustn't forget to iron my jacket for work tomorrow… '

Q: Have you experienced these kinds of mental interruptions?

Q: What ideas do you have for dealing with this problem?

3 Knowing what to pray for

You've found time and space to pray and you're ready to start. But how do you decide what to pray for today?

Q: What are the good points in how you choose what to pray about? And what are the bad points?

Read
Romans 8:26,27.

Q: What does Paul mean when he says the Spirit intercedes for us?

Prayer

Start by reading out loud Proverbs 2:1–6:

My child, listen to me and treasure my instructions. Tune your ears to wisdom, and concentrate on understanding. Cry out for insight and understanding. Search for them as you would for lost money or hidden treasure. Then you will understand what it means to fear the Lord, and you will gain knowledge of God. For the Lord grants wisdom! From his mouth come knowledge and understanding.

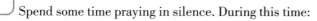 Spend some time praying in silence. During this time:

- thank God for the gift of prayer and the good things it brings us
- pray for your own prayer life
- give thanks for the good prayer experiences you've had
- say sorry for the times you don't pray when you should
- ask for help if you have particular problems with your prayer life

Share together some of your responses to these verses within the group and pray for each other.

En Route

Make a list of the things you could pray for:

- your Christian friends and family
- your non-Christian friends, family and work colleagues
- your church and community
- people and events in the news
- yourself

Begin to use this list when you pray on your own.

Think about using the list to pray with others. You could arrange to meet up with one or two others as prayer partners or a prayer triplet and pray together regularly – weekly or fortnightly – for the people and situations on all your lists.

Further Afield

1 ELEMENTS

Read

Luke 11:1–4

Q: The disciples want help with prayer. What does Jesus describe here as elements to include when they pray?

Q: Which of these do you remember to include in your prayers? And which do you tend to leave out?

These verses are the foundation of perhaps the most familiar of all prayers. When we know something very well, it's easy to say it almost without thinking, to recite it rather than pray it.

Finish by praying the Lord's Prayer – slowly. Leave a short gap between each sentence and reflect on what you've just said.

2 ATTITUDES

Read

Luke 11:5–10

Q: What kind of attitude to prayer did Jesus want to encourage by telling this story?

Q: What happens when you don't get an immediate answer to your prayers? Do you keep on going or are you easily discouraged?

Q: How can we encourage one another to keep on praying and not give up?

Q: What do you need to keep on praying for at the moment? Pray for those things now.

3 GIFTS

Read

Luke 11:11–13

Q: Think about gifts you've received. What do you think is the best gift you've ever had?

Q: Why do we give gifts to one another? God doesn't wait for a particular time of year or a special event to give gifts. Why do you think God gives us gifts?

Q: What kind of gifts does God want to give us, his children?

List the gifts God has given you and thank him for them. Think about how can you use them to serve him.

3   *Prayer and other people*

Setting Out

Spontaneous ... formal ... relaxed ... silent ... spoken together ... read from ancient texts ... Prayer with others can take many forms. Some of these are experiences we find easy or familiar. Others may be scary, challenging, stressful. So much depends on our personalities, and on our experiences to date.

When we're in church, we may barely notice that there are other people praying along with us, but in a small fellowship group or with one or two others we can be all too aware of everyone else. For some, praying aloud with others is an edgy, uncomfortable experience. Others find it immensely rewarding and exciting.

Whatever kind of prayer with others you're used to, and however you feel about it, the Bible is clear that it's an essential part of our lives.

Alongside our experiences of praying *with* others, is our experience of praying *for* others. That, too, isn't always as easy as it sounds. So often our prayers for others, like our prayers for ourselves maybe, are just a long list of needs and problems that we want God to sort out. Just *how* should we be praying for one another?

So, setting aside the generalities, how do *you* feel about prayer?

For each statement below, choose which answer best expresses your feelings about prayer.

1   I find it easiest to pray

     a. on my own
     b. in church during a service
     c. with a few others, eg as part of a small group or with a prayer partner
     d. I find it very hard to pray anywhere
     e. I always find it easy to pray

2   When I pray I prefer to use

     a. traditional prayers eg part of a service
     b. prayers someone else has written eg from a book or Bible reading notes

c. my own words

d. silence

e. I like to vary it each time

3 When someone says, 'Let's pray' I think

    a. about something else.

    b. 'Oh no, not again.'

    c. 'Great. Let's do it.'

    d. 'You pray, I'll listen.'

    e. 'Help, I don't know what to say.'

4 Praying with others is

    a. fun

    b. a rare event

    c. very rewarding

    d. a struggle

    e. a new idea

5 Praying with others leaves me feeling

    a. closer to God

    b. a failure

    c. uncomfortable

    d. refreshed

    e. as though it was a waste of time

 After you've had time to consider, discuss your answers together.

Signposts

1 Praying with others

Q: When do you pray with others?

Q: What do you find most helpful when you do? And most difficult?

Read

Matthew 18:19,20

Acts 12:1–12

Q: What reasons can you find in these passages for praying with others?

Q: Can you think of times you've experienced these benefits?

Q: What other benefits come from praying with other people?

Q: Why do you think some people find praying out loud in a service or small group intimidating or difficult?

Q: How do you feel about praying aloud in front of other people? Why?

Q: How can a group, of any size, help those who are uncertain or afraid of praying aloud to take part?

2 Praying for others

Q: One Sunday your church leader asks you all to pray for someone you have never met. What can make it difficult to pray for people we don't know?

In the New Testament there are many descriptions of prayer for others. Paul's letters include some of his prayers for the churches he wrote to; some of these he knew well and others he only knew second-hand, through the reports of others. His prayers give us insight into how we too can pray for others.

Read

Colossians 1:3,4,7–12

Paul had never met the people of the Colossian church but still had many things he wanted to pray for them.

Q: How does Paul begin his prayers for the church?

Using verses 10–12, make a list of the things Paul asks God to do for the Colossian Christians.

Q: Why do you think he includes these things in his prayers for the church?

Think about your own prayers for other people.

- How often do you give thanks for good things you see in them?
- How much of your prayers are for things of temporary benefit, eg for health, relationships and practical needs?
- How much of your prayers ask for things that would have an eternal benefit, things that will build up their relationship with God?

Q: How could you develop the way you pray for others?

Prayer

Write down the following three headings on a separate sheet of paper:

- National and international news
- The worldwide Church
- Our local community and church(es)

Spend a few minutes thinking of things that you could pray for under each of these headings and jot them down.

Once you have several ideas for each heading, choose just one from each category and commit to pray regularly for each of those three things over the next few weeks. If you don't know much about a particular situation but would like to pray for it, then think about how to find out more about it.

For this exercise use a large sheet of paper or a flipchart that everyone can see. In your group, you'll need to agree on the three things you're praying for so that you all pray for the same things. Pray both as a group and on your own, through the week.

Pray for the three things you've chosen, either praying silently, or writing down your prayers or praying aloud.

Finally, pray for each other, using the words of Paul in Colossians 1:9–12. As you read this together, pray those words for the people sitting immediately next to you. Go on praying for those people this week.

We ask God to give you a complete understanding of what he wants to do in your lives, and we ask him to make you wise with spiritual wisdom. Then the way you live will always honour and please the Lord, and you will continually do good, kind things for others. All the while, you will learn to know God better and better.

En Route

Using a prayer journal

A prayer journal is simply a written account of your prayer life. At its most straightforward it's a list of the things you pray for each day, with space for anything God said to you during that prayer time and a note of answers you receive. Some people also like to write out their prayers as they pray them. Others develop the idea further by including things such as what they've read from the Bible with thoughts and comments on it, or include reflections on sermons, books read, conversations etc that are relevant in some way. Some people use the journal every day, others at times of particular significance.

A prayer journal can help your prayer life in several ways:

- Improved concentration.
- Encouragement to be specific. It's much easier to see when a prayer has been answered if you prayed specifically rather than in vague generalities; it also encourages you to think of real words instead of the 'errs' and 'ums'.
- A record. A journal is there to look back on as time goes on. You can see how you have grown and changed, how God has answered your prayers and worked in your life. This can be a real encouragement to keep on going, especially through difficult times.
- Don't forget though that everyone's different. A prayer journal doesn't

automatically make you more holy than someone who doesn't keep one or make your prayers more meaningful and effective. If journals aren't for you then don't lie awake at night worrying about it! Pray in a way that suits you.

Further Afield

1 HYPOCRISY

Read

Matthew 6:1–6

Q: Why was Jesus so critical of the hypocrites?

Q: Why do you think the hypocrites prayed in public?

We could assume from verse 6 that we should only pray in private, but the rest of the Bible makes it clear that this isn't the case. So, it wasn't really the public prayer Jesus didn't like, but the showing off that went with it. The hypocrites were only interested in making a good impression on other people, instead of concentrating on God.

Q: When you pray with others, how much do you worry about what they're thinking of your prayer?

Q: Do you ever fall into the trap of praying to impress others?

Q: How can we avoid such a situation?

2 UNITY

Read

John 17:1–26

Q: This is Jesus' prayer for his disciples and for all of us who would come to know and serve him. What does Jesus ask God to do for his followers? Why does he want these things to happen?

Q: How often do you pray for unity with your brothers and sisters in Christ?

Unity isn't just about working with other churches. It begins with our own relationships with other Christians. Do you need to put right a relationship? Think about how God would want you to try and sort this out and ask that he will help you to do that this week.

3 RESPONSE

Read

Acts 12:1–19

The Church was suffering. King Herod Agrippa had killed James, one of the original disciples, and had Peter arrested, presumably so he too could be executed.

Q: How did the Church respond to this crisis?

Q: Their prayers led to a miraculous release for Peter, but how did they respond when he turned up at their prayer meeting?

Q: Why do you think they didn't believe that the person at the door could really be Peter?

This story reminds us that God can do amazing things when we pray, however hopeless the situation may seem. However, it also shows us that we can only see a part of the picture. This story begins with James' death and gives us no clues to the reasons why God released Peter but left James to die.

4 *Difficult decisions*

When we travel, we usually rely on being able to see the way ahead. But what if we can't? When darkness comes there are some practical things we can do. If we're driving we can turn on the car lights and stick to well-lit roads. On foot we can take a torch. But there are times when severe weather conditions make travel so difficult we are stuck at home – or in a lay-by!

There are some special situations where people don't necessarily need to be able to see the way ahead to move forward in the right direction. Pilots, for example, can use hi-tech systems to navigate planes through darkness and bad weather.

Unfortunately we can't flick switches and turn on automatic systems to navigate successfully through life, even if we'd want to rely on temperamental computer chips. God knows everything that lies ahead of us. Our problem is finding out how he wants us to go forward.

Setting Out

What kind of decision-maker are you? Choose the answer that fits you best.

1 You've been unexpectedly invited to a surprise party tonight. How do you decide what to wear?

   a. I plan carefully and shop ahead so I know there's always something suitable in my wardrobe.

   b. Great, a chance to buy something new. I'm spending the rest of the day prowling round the shops.

   c. I'm pretty sure I'll wear the red. Or maybe the blue. Or should it be the black? Or the long-sleeves? Maybe the red would be best after all. What do you think?

   d. I just have time to make sure my one suit is pressed and that'll have to do.

   e. I'm all right as I am, aren't I?

   f. Something else? What?

2 You've arrived on holiday and it's the first full day. How do you like to decide what to do today?

   a. You planned every moment of every day weeks ago and you've brought the list with you.

   b. You've made a list of all the things you'd like to do but you'll see how you feel before you decide which one to choose today.

   c. You don't know what there is to do but you've picked up some tourist leaflets and you'll read them over breakfast.

   d. You never make decisions like that. You'll just set off and see what happens.

   e. You've made a decision. You're going to do nothing today. And probably tomorrow. And the next day. You might change your mind. You'll see how it goes. Maybe.

   f. Something else? What?

3 You're trying to decide whether to apply for a new job. Do you...

   a. Write long lists of pros and cons and weigh them up for weeks first?

   b. Make a decision. Then make a different final decision. Then go back to the first one and eventually go with the decision you made just before time ran out?

   c. Go with your gut feeling. If it feels good, do it?

   d. Ask everyone you know. Worry about the conflicting advice you've received. Then resort to a, b or c anyway?

   e. Pray. And pray some more. And pray again. And then go with one of the other options.

   f. Something else? What?

Q: Do you think you make good decisions or not? Why?

Share your answers with one another. Can you learn from the way others approach decisions?

Signposts

Six ways to seek God's guidance

1 Read the Bible

Read

Joshua 1:8

Q: This verse says we should meditate on the Bible day and night. What do you think this means?

Q: Why will this help us know what God wants us to do?

Q: Not every difficult situation we face is mentioned in the Bible. So, how can a knowledge of the Bible still help us?

2 Listen for God's 'still small voice'

Read

John 10:2–5

Q: How do the sheep know which is the right man to follow?

Q: The shepherd calls the sheep by name. What does this say about his relationship with them?

Read

Deuteronomy 13:4
Isaiah 30:21

Q: We need to be able to pick out God's voice so we can follow it. How do you think we could learn to do this?

Hearing God speak hardly ever means hearing an audible voice. God's voice might be 'heard' as a persistent thought, a feeling, an inner sense of rightness or a growing understanding of God's reasons for a particular way forward. The risk is that we make mistakes; we believe we've heard God speak to us when we haven't. Paul says, '...test everything that is said...'
(1 Thessalonians 5:21). We need to check out what we've heard to make sure it's from God. Does it pass these tests?

- Does it agree with the Bible? (2 Timothy 3:16)
- Does it show love for others? (1 Corinthians13:4)
- Does it strengthen and encourage others in some way? (Ephesians 4:12)
- Do we know God's peace? (Philippians 4:6,7)

If it fails any of the first three tests then we can be sure it wasn't God speaking to us. Knowing God's peace is harder to measure but its presence or absence is a good pointer to the right way forward.

3 Through supernatural events

These are dramatic moments that leave little room for doubt about God's plans, but are just one of the ways God speaks to us – however much we might wish he would use them every time.

Check out how God spoke to:

Samuel in 1 Samuel 3:1–10
Peter in Acts 12:7, 9
Joseph in Matthew 2:12,13,19,22
Paul in Acts 16:6–10

Q: We can't assume that God will never speak to us in any of these ways but we shouldn't rely on it. What do you think are the risks of spending too much time looking for miraculous signs?

4 Ask other people

Read
Proverbs 12:15; 10:14; 11:2,9,12,18; 15:14
Psalm 111:10

Q: What characteristics should we look for in a person before taking advice from them?

Q: Who do you go to for advice? Why?

Read

Acts 21:10–14

Q: Why don't the believers want Paul to go to Jerusalem?

Q: Why didn't Paul take their advice?

Q: What can Paul's experiences teach us about taking advice from others?

5 Use your common sense

Read

Proverbs 4:5
James 1:5

Sometimes we try to 'overspiritualise' decisions, praying when really we already know the answer. We may know exactly what the Bible teaches already. We may have responsibilities and commitments we should fulfil. We shouldn't ignore the common sense God has given us!

6 Prayer - the most vital step of all

Read

1 Corinthians 2:16
Philippians 2:5

Q: How will prayer help us know how God wants us to live?

Q: Have you experienced God guiding you in one of these six ways?

Share some of your experiences with one another.

Q: You've sought God's guidance in every possible way but still feel you've no clear answer. However, the moment of truth has arrived – the decision needs to be made NOW. What do you do?

Prayer

Q: Are there areas of your life or decisions you are facing where you are looking for God's guidance at the moment? What could help you find it?

Q: Are there areas of your life or decisions you are facing where you are aware that you are ignoring God's guidance at the moment? Why?

Pray for the situations in your lives where you need to know God's guidance or find the strength to obey him. Also pray for situations where God's guidance is needed in the life of your church, community and in the wider world. Don't forget to pray for the three things you chose in the last session.

End by reading these verses from Psalm 143:8–10 as a prayer:

Let me hear of your unfailing love to me in the morning,
* for I am trusting you.*
Show me where to walk,
* for I have come to you in prayer.*
Save me from my enemies, Lord;
* I run to you to hide me.*
Teach me to do your will,
* for you are my God.*
May your gracious Spirit lead me forward
* on a firm footing.*

Further Afield

1 BIG DECISIONS
Read
Luke 6:12–16

Q: Why did Jesus go off to pray on this occasion?

Q: Think back to a recent decision you made. How much time did you spend praying about it?

Q: Is there a decision or problem looming on your horizon at the moment? Pray about it now. Why not plan to put aside some extra time this week to pray for this?

2 UNEXPECTED DETOURS

Read
Acts 16:6–10

Q: How did Paul know he shouldn't be going to Asia as he had originally planned?

Q: What led him to Macedonia instead?

Q: Our plans don't always work out as we expected. Proverbs 16:9 says, 'We can make our plans, but the Lord determines our steps'. When your plans don't work out, how do you react?

Q: What can we learn from Paul's experience that will help us when our plans change?

Pray for yourself or other people you know about who are finding that their plans aren't working out as they hoped. What do they need most in this situation?

3 THE CHALLENGE OF TRUST

Read

Psalm 37:5

Q:In the NIV this verse is translated, 'Commit your way to the LORD; trust in him and he will do this'. What does it mean to commit your way to the Lord?

Q:Do you trust in him? What does this mean for you at the moment?

Some of you might like to share your current struggles or joys in trusting God, followed by prayer together.

Read the verse again then sit silently for a few minutes allowing God to speak to you through it. If you find it hard to concentrate, say the verse again and return to silence. Write down anything God says to you during this time.

5 *Fasting*

Watch the TV almost any day of the week and somewhere in the schedules you'll find a cookery programme of some kind. Look in the bestseller lists and you'll see books full of recipes by chefs that are household names. Adverts, magazines, newspaper articles… food is everywhere!

Jesus too thought food was important. Several of his miracles involved meals in some way. He cooked breakfast for his disciples, and spent a lot of his time sharing meals with all kinds of people. However, sometimes food took a back seat. The Bible also speaks about fasting – the decision to avoid food for the benefit of our relationship with God. Is fasting something that should be consigned to history, left to the super-keen or is it something we should be doing today?

Q: In what circumstances do people fast today and what are they hoping to achieve?

Q: Are any of these your first reaction to the idea of fasting yourself?
- You must be joking!
- How do I start?
- It's bad enough trying to lose weight!
- Do I have to?
- I like my food too much.
- What a brilliant idea!
- How can I get out of this one?

Signposts

1 Jesus and fasting

Read

Matthew 6:16–18; 9:14,15

Q: The Pharisees fasted twice a week and John's disciples had followed this pattern. Why didn't Jesus' disciples fast like the others?

Q: What evidence can you find from reading these verses that we should fast?

Q: Is there anything here that suggests we don't need to fast?

Q: Does Jesus give any indication of how often someone should fast? Why/why not?

Q: Why do you think many churches say very little about fasting?

2 Why fast?

There are many descriptions of people fasting throughout the Bible. Read these passages and make a note of who was fasting and why.

Read

Judges 20:24–28
Jonah 3:3–10
1 Samuel 31:11–13
2 Samuel 1:11,12
Ezra 8:21–23
Matthew 4:1,2
Acts 13:2,3
Acts 14:23

Q: Like prayer, fasting is not an automatic route to the 'results' we are hoping for. Psalm 35:13 says, 'Yet when they were ill, I grieved for them. I even fasted and prayed for them, but my prayers returned unanswered'. So how would you sum up the benefits of fasting?

Q: Look back at Matthew 6:16–18. Why did Jesus criticise the hypocrites for fasting? What do you think this means for us when we fast?

3 What does fasting involve?

Fasting usually involves giving up food for a period of time for a spiritual purpose. The Bible describes three usual levels of fasting.

a The normal fast

Read

Matthew 4:2

Jesus is described here as eating nothing, but as his fast lasted for 40 days we can assume that he did drink water. This is the usual form of fasting. A normal fast can be for anything from missing one meal to taking no food for the body's limit of around 40 days. Some people will reach their maximum limit sooner than others. Any length of fast, if carried out for the right reasons, will be of some benefit.

b The partial fast

Read

Daniel 10:1–3

Q: Depending on what is given up, a partial fast may be continued without limit. What did Daniel give up here?

Q: How does this kind of fast differ from going on a diet?

c The absolute fast

Read

Esther 4:15,16
Acts 9:8,9

Q: How is this kind of fast different from the others?

This is the fast with the most limited maximum timespan and the most risks. It's not for beginners! Undertaking a fast which excludes all fluids including water is very unusual and potentially very dangerous. These were extreme fasts in extreme situations.

There is one other kind of fast mentioned in the Bible and that is a **supernatural fast**. Deuteronomy 9:9 describes Moses as saying, 'That was when I was on the mountain receiving the tablets of stone inscribed with the covenant that the Lord had made with you. I was there for forty days and forty nights, and all that time I ate nothing and drank no water.' No one could normally survive without water for that length of time. Moses was called onto the mountain and miraculously sustained there by God.

> **Remember!** In general, food fasts aren't recommended for diabetics, pregnant women and others with certain medical conditions. If you have any doubts, take medical advice first.

Non-food fasts

Read
Daniel 6:16–18
Daniel 10:3

Q: What do the King and Daniel give up that isn't food in these verses?

Q: Why do you think they fasted from these things?

The principle of fasting could be applied to other areas of our lives as well as food, although this isn't a biblical requirement or a replacement for food fasts but an added extra possibility!

Q: What else might someone choose to fast from? Why?

Q: Is there something that you might benefit from giving up for a short time?

Q: Think back over the various Bible verses you've read. How is it suggested we should spend the time we've saved through not sitting down for a meal or not spending the evening watching TV?

Prayer

Pray you would develop a deeper relationship with God.

 End by praying Ephesians 3:16–19 together for one another:

I pray that from his glorious, unlimited resources he will give you mighty inner strength through his Holy Spirit. And I pray that Christ will be more and more at home in your hearts as you trust in him. May your roots go down deep into the soil of God's marvellous love. And may you have the power to understand, as all God's people should, how wide, how long, how high, and how deep his love really is. May you experience the love of Christ, though it is so great you will never fully understand it. Then you will be filled with the fullness of life and power that comes from God.

En Route

Consider trying a partial 24-hour fast or a short fast that means you miss a single meal sometime this week. Use the missed mealtime(s) as an extra opportunity to pray and worship. If you can't pray during the mealtime then find another time in the day.

Think about: What is the best day for you? Are there things you might need to organise in advance? If you normally share this meal with others, don't feel you have to go over the top in disguising your fast; don't pretend you feel ill to avoid the meal, for example. There's a difference between broadcasting your decision to fast so you look good, and sharing your decision because you have to, or encouraging others by sharing the benefits you found from doing it.

Further Afield

1 Food for the soul

Read

Isaiah 55:1–3

Q: What do these verses from Isaiah say God offers us?

Q: What do we have to do to receive these things?

Spending time listening to God can be very hard. For some of us, just sitting still is difficult! For others, it's hard to put aside the concerns of the day. Sometimes it's almost impossible to find somewhere to pray that won't be interrupted and for some it may be a new idea that we should listen and not just speak to God.

Q: Do you try to spend time listening to God, as well as speaking to him? What do you find most difficult about doing this?

Perhaps more than anything else, listening prayer requires practice. Don't be too ambitious, but try to spend a few minutes in silence with God now. You may find it useful to look back at the ideas for coping with 'mental drift' that you came up with in chapter 2.

2 Picturing God

Read
Psalm 62:5–8

Q: How do these verses describe God?

Q: Which of these pictures or characteristics of God do you find most encouraging at the moment?

Spend some time quietly before God now. You might want to begin by thinking about the description of God you've just chosen. Why did you choose that one in particular? What does it mean for you? Try to listen to God. What does he want to say to you today?

Share in your group your thoughts on the picture of God that most encourages you, and try to say why it does.

3 Spread before God

Read

2 Kings 19:9–19

Q: How did Hezekiah deal with the letter he received?

Q: Why do you think he spread it out before God while he prayed?

Q: Some people use physical objects when they pray eg photos, letters, candles, a cross... Why do you think they would find this helpful?

Q: Have you ever tried doing this? Why?

Think about whether it would be helpful for you to use objects in prayer. For example, could you find something that reminds you of one of the aspects of God's character you've been thinking about?

6 *In the tough times*

Setting Out

In the face of a desperate situation, many people turn to prayer. Oh God, help me… heal them… put it right… make it different… We cry out for God to change things, to put things back the way they were, to fix it so everything is all right.

Not everyone always feels able to do this, though. Sometimes things are so bad that we can't pray at all, we don't have the energy or the desire and God seems very far away. It might be that we feel unable to pray because we have nothing positive to say, or we are filled with blazing anger or desperate sadness and we're not sure that we can express these things to God. However we deal with difficult times we can be sure of one thing: they're going to happen to us sooner or later.

So, how do *you* respond? Choose the answer that seems most like you.

When life is tough I usually…

- pray more than usual / about the same as usual / less than usual / don't pray at all
- seek help and support from others / keep things the same / hide the problem / run away
- go to church more often / it doesn't change / go less / drop out altogether
- find that being a Christian is what keeps me going / don't think it makes much difference / find that it actually makes things more difficult / I'm not a Christian anyway

Q: Why do you think you respond in this way?

 Discuss your answers together.

Signposts

Read

2 Corinthians 12:6–10
Matthew 26:36–46
Jonah 2:1 – 3:3
2 Samuel 12:7–23; Psalm 51:1–4

You might like to divide up into pairs or smaller groups and share these passages out. When you've finished, discuss your ideas with one another.

In each of these passages someone is facing a difficult time. For each one, answer these questions:

Q: What kind of suffering was this person facing?

Q: How did this make them feel?

Q: What did they do about it?

Q: How did God respond to them?

Q: What was their final response to God?

Q: When you face difficult times and pray about them, what are you hoping will happen?

Q: In how many of the situations you've just looked at did the person get the answer they wanted?

It's often said that prayer changes things and in the Bible we find many occasions when prayer led to victory in battle, to healing, changed circumstances, even resurrection from the dead. However, in these situations that we've just looked at, it didn't always appear that prayer had changed anything. Despite their prayers Paul was still ill, Jesus died on the cross and David's child died.

These experiences make it clear that prayer is not a magic wand that will automatically save us from disaster or suffering, so just what does it achieve? Read again 2 Corinthians 12:6–10. Here we find clues to help us see what does happen when we pray.

Q: In verses 8 and 9 Paul tells us that he prayed three times, asking God to change his circumstances by taking away the 'thorn in his flesh' – but it didn't happen. So what did Paul receive from God by praying?

Paul's prayers weren't pointless. As he prayed he found that – although his circumstances didn't change – he did. He began to see his life through God's eyes instead of through his own. Through his prayers, God brought him the encouragement he needed to cope with the difficult situation he found himself in.

David Augsberger in an article on grieving found in *The Complete Book of Everyday Christianity* (IVP ed Robert Banks and R Paul Stevens, 1997) says, 'God is our help, not our escape. He walks with us through pain rather than waltzes us out of it'.

Q: Have you experienced this truth?

Q: How did God help you in those difficult times?

Q: Paul also found that his prayers brought him some understanding of why he was suffering. What reason did Paul see for the 'thorn'?

Suffering and difficult circumstances can be caused by our own actions. Jonah wouldn't have been shipwrecked if he had gone directly to Nineveh; David would not have been grieving for his child if he hadn't committed adultery and murder. Sometimes through suffering we learn lessons or develop our character in ways that make us more like Jesus.

However, suffering is not always 'our fault'.

Read

Luke 13:1–5

Q: Did these people deserve to die?

Q: What led to their deaths?

Jesus had clearly done nothing to deserve his suffering either. Their experiences remind us that God always has a reason for allowing bad things to happen to us, but we can't see the full picture in the way that he can. 'My thoughts are completely different from yours … And my ways are far beyond anything you could imagine' (Isaiah 55:8). We may come to understand why something is happening to us, as Paul did. Or, like Job, we may not.

But when everything gets really tough, is it alright to tell God how I really feel?

Read

Psalm 13:1,2
Job 7:6–16

Q: How would you describe the way David and Job spoke to God?

Q: Why might it be important for us to be honest in our dealings with God?

Sometimes things can be so bad that we are unable to pray at all: we are too ill, too worried, too unhappy or too angry with God to find the words or maybe God seems to have gone away and left us to it, we can't sense his presence at all.

Q: Have you ever experienced times like this, when you can't pray at all?

Four ideas for the really tough times

1 Rely on the Holy Spirit

Read

Romans 8:26,27

Q: How can the Holy Spirit help us when we can't pray for ourselves?

2 Wait on God

Read

Psalm 46:10,11
Isaiah 40:29–31

Q: How do these verses suggest we spend time with God?

Q: What does God promise us when we do this?

3 Express your feelings visibly rather than in words

Read

John 11:32,33
Psalm 56:8

Q: How did Mary show her feelings to Jesus?

Q: How does God respond to us in these times?

4 Ask others to pray for you

Read

Philippians 1:12–19

Q: Why might this be a hard thing to do?

Q: How about you? Do you ask others to pray for you in difficult times? Why/why not?

Prayer

Q: Are you facing a difficult situation at the moment? Consider sharing that situation with others, so they can pray for you.

Use this prayer, taken from Psalm 13. Read out the verses in italic type. Between each set of verses, spend a few minutes in silence following the suggestion for private prayer.

O Lord, how long will you forget me? Forever?
  How long will you look the other way?
How long must I struggle with anguish in my soul,
  with sorrow in my heart every day?
How long will my enemy have the upper hand?

Spend time expressing your feelings to God, perhaps over a difficult situation you are facing, or that faced by someone you know well.

Turn and answer me, O Lord my God!
  Restore the light to my eyes, or I will die.
Don't let my enemies gloat, saying, 'We have defeated him!'
  Don't let them rejoice at my downfall.

Tell God what you would like him to do in this situation.

But I trust in your unfailing love.
  I will rejoice because you have rescued me.

Make the decision to trust God whatever lies ahead.

I will sing to the Lord because he has been so good to me.

Give thanks for the good things he gives you or praise him for the good things in his character.

En Route

Start a prayer chain

Some groups and churches have prayer chains, which provide immediate prayer support for particular situations. People who join the chain give their phone number to the organiser. When a prayer need arises, it is passed to that organiser who then rings the first person in the chain. They then ring the next person on the list, who rings the person after them and so on. To allow for people being out, each person usually keeps on going through the list until they find someone in (rather than leaving messages that might not be picked up for some time). The person in charge needs to be wise about how much information to give out to the others in the chain, but even scanty details of a situation can lead to effective prayer support.

If no such chain exists in your group, church or area, why not consider starting one? You could offer to pray for people who aren't part of the chain as well as those who are.

Further Afield

1 Worry

Read
Philippians 4:6
John 14:27

Q: It's not easy to imagine never being worried about anything. Do you see yourself as a worrier or are you a laid-back kind of person?

Q: How does Paul say we should deal with our problems?

These verses don't say that God will always take away our problems if we pray. Neither do they say that we should pretend everything is all right really. We can be honest about the difficulties we face. However, they do promise that God will give us his peace in the midst of difficulty and suffering.

Q: Are you worrying about something at the moment? Pray that God will give you his peace now.

2 Grief

Read

John 11:32–36
2 Corinthians 1:3,4
Matthew 11:28–30

Q: How did Jesus react to Mary's grief at the death of Lazarus?

God is not distant from our pain, he understands how we feel and grieves alongside us. However, he can offer us even more than that – he offers us his comfort and hope.

Q: Can you think of difficult times in your life when you have experienced God's comfort?

Give thanks for the times God has comforted you. Pray that God will bring comfort and hope to you or others who need it at the moment.

3 Growth

Read

Isaiah 40:29–31

Q: Think back over the time you've been looking at your prayer life. Do you think it has developed over that time? How?

Q: What is the most significant thing you've learnt?

Q: As we read these words of Isaiah, what do they promise those who spend time with God?

Be still before God and reflect on these verses now.

About the author

Kate Hayes, born into a non-churchgoing family in Sheffield, decided to become a Christian aged 12 after being 'dragged along' to a Pathfinder meeting by a friend. After studying Psychology at university, she did teacher training but then found herself working in bookshops and in software testing for the book trade. Since 1994 she's been in Dukinfield, Greater Manchester, where she co-ordinates and writes materials for small groups at St John's Church.

OTHER TITLES by KATE HAYES
THE RE:ACTION SERIES – 6 SMALL GROUP RESOURCES

For the tough times
Does God care when I'm hurting?
ISBN 1 85999 622 1

Chosen for change
Am I part of God's big plan?
ISBN 1 85999 623 X

The possibility of purpose
What's the meaning of my life?
ISBN 1 85999 620 5

Jesus: the sequel
Is he really coming back?
ISBN 1 85999 621 3

More than fine words
Does my faith impact 24/7?
ISBN 1 85999 770 8

More than bricks and ritual
Am I a team player for God?
ISBN 1 85999 769 4

Available from all good Christian bookshops or from Scripture Union Mail Order: PO Box 5148, Milton Keynes MLO, MK2 2YX, tel 08450 706 006, or online through www.scriptureunion.org.uk

SCRIPTURE UNION
USING THE BIBLE TO INSPIRE CHILDREN, YOUNG PEOPLE AND ADULTS TO KNOW GOD